WALKING THROUGH THE VALLEY

Grieving Well One Step at a Time

C.S. Boddie

Meadowlark Press/ Littleton

All rights reserved. No part of this publication may be reproduced, distributed or transmitted in any form or by any means, without prior written permission.

C.S. Boddie/Meadowlark Press, LLC
12339 W. Burgundy Avenue
Littleton, CO 80127
www.Meadowlark-Press.com

Publisher's Note: The information in this book is true and complete to the best of our knowledge. It is offered without guarantee on the part of the author or Meadowlark Press. The author and Meadowlark Press disclaim all liability in connection with the use of this book.

Book Layout © 2014 BookDesignTemplates.com

Walking Through the Valley/ C.S. Boddie -- 1st Edition.

Print Edition ISBN 978-1-7336621-0-9/ Ebook Edition ISBN 978-1-7336621-1-6

Front cover and all images on internal pages by C.S. Boddie, except where credited differently.

Library of Congress ECPN applied for.

Dedicated to All the Brokenhearted

He comforts us in all our troubles so that we can comfort others.

—2 Corinthians 1:4 NLT

CONTENTS

Foreword•ix
Introduction•1
Walk One, Day One•8
Walk Two, Day Two•10
Walk Three, Day Three•12
Walk Four, Day Four•14
Walk Five, Day Five•16
Walk Six, Day Six•18
Walk Seven, Day Seven•22
Walk Eight, Day Eight•24
Walk Nine, Day Nine•26
Walk Ten, Day Ten•28
Walk Eleven, Day Eleven•30
Walk Twelve, Day Twelve•32
Walk Thirteen, Day Thirteen•34
Walk Fourteen, Day Fourteen•36
Walk Fifteen, Day Fifteen•38
Walk Sixteen, Day Sixteen•40
Walk Seventeen, Day Seventeen•42
Walk Eighteen, Day Eighteen•44
Walk Nineteen, Day Nineteen•46
Walk Twenty, Day Twenty•48
Walk Twenty One, Day Twenty One•50
Afterword•53

Grief is like a fingerprint, unique for each person and each loss, even though there are stages in the grieving process that are universal.

FOREWORD

This beautiful book is a guidebook for the unique and yet universal experience of grief. C.S. Boddie speaks with the authentic voice of one who knows first-hand the experience of unspeakable loss. And yet it is not her voice the sojourner hears most clearly; it is the still Voice that lights every nook and cranny of the darkest path. Whether you have lost a dream or a dearly loved one, this is a must-have companion for the tangled trails of grief.

—Sharon Hersh MA, LPC

Ms. Hersh is a licensed professional counselor and the author of numerous published books. Also, she is an adjunct professor in counseling classes at several seminaries and a popular speaker at retreats and conferences. Ms. Hersh lives in Lone Tree, Colorado, and can be contacted through her website, www.sharonhersh.com, or on Facebook.

Grief is like a long valley, a winding valley where any bend may reveal a totally new landscape.

— C.S. Lewis

INTRODUCTION

After a few trips through the valley of grief, I found myself on a mountain path with a heart that had been broken again. It was then I rediscovered how walking could be very healing.

I had lived through many losses in my life—more than some people have, fewer than others do—and regular walks and hikes had already surprised me with beauty, peace and a totally new landscape, in familiar places.

This time I realized that walking while grieving was like wandering off a worn path to smell a rose; a few extra steps took me to soul-filling beauty and allowed me space. Even though they were often bittersweet, these walks soothed my spirit and helped me make sense of the new realities of my life. Essentially, my soul was restored with each step I took.

Also, I recognized that walking enabled me to function better in my everyday life by helping me carve out a little time just for grieving and it helped me mitigate loneliness and avoid depression.

Eventually, I felt led to share what I'd discovered with other people who are grieving. As I explored the idea and started writing, the project evolved to include Scripture as well as quotes, and links to music videos and other resources. It ended up being a devotional.

Walking Through the Valley is that devotional. It's meant to be a friend who comes alongside you right where you are in your grief journey, walks with you and then enables you to continue walking after you're done with the book. It can be used daily for three weeks—there are 21 devotions—or now and again over a longer time, and you can use it repeatedly.

Why walk through grief?

In my experience, which has been confirmed by what others have said and written, walking is a great tool when you're grieving.

How? Well, for one thing, as you walk you move through time and space on your own power. In that way, it helps you feel normal for a while, when life feels anything but. Also, as you put one foot in front of the other, your mind is freed to work things out about a loss or losses and resulting changes in your life.

Plus, the physical exercise of walking enables you to manage the stress of grieving (Yay, endorphins!) and enhances your fitness. And a couple more things: walking in nature—urban parks do qualify—can keep you from slipping into clinical depression; while walking with a friend, either human or canine, can help you better cope with loneliness.

Here are a few tips for using this devotional and walking while grieving:

- Read each devotion before you walk every day.
- Make time for walks; that is, schedule them in and reserve the time just for you.
- Go to the resources in the devotions; they may enhance your experience. (No links in the print book, so please just search the resources yourself online.)
- Sit and write for 15 minutes at the beginning or end of your walks in a journal.
- Bring along your phone or a camera to take photos or bring a sketchbook and pencils.
- Feel free to use this book in your own way.

Finding time to walk

It can be tough to find time to walk in busy schedules, but thinking outside the box can help. How about early morning, before bed at night, on your lunch hour or even before getting into the car to drive home after work?

About grief

Grief is like a fingerprint, unique for each person and each loss, even though there are stages in the grieving process that are universal.

Some losses are grieved quickly. More-traumatic losses one may never get over fully; they are really just integrated into one's life. When grief goes on and on; it may be "complicated grief," and require counseling.

Ordinarily, though, a person can grieve on his or her own with the Lord's help and comfort. Support groups where the bereaved can share with others may help too.

The purpose here is not to go into the grieving process in detail. Please go to the many good books and articles that describe it in detail. (See Resources.)

Finally, it's worth mentioning that we all experience many types of losses that merit grieving: deaths, divorce, unemployment, loss of good health for ourselves or for family members, broken relationships and others. This devotional can be used to grieve various losses—separately or simultaneously—though the language in the devotions leans toward loss through death.

Now, as we come to the end of this introduction, Dear Reader, and you get ready to begin, know that you have my deepest sympathies on your losses; I mean, I feel for you.

~~~

I thought I could describe a state; make a map of sorrow. Sorrow, however, turns out to be not a state, but a process.

— C.S. Lewis

I don't move away from grief, rather through it.

— Taya Kyle

RESOURCES

Articles

Children

"Grief and Children," American Academy of Childhood & Adolescent Psychiatry

"Helping Kids Grieve," SesameStreetinCommunities.org

"How to Help Your Child Grieve," by Candy Arrington, Focus on the Family.com

General

"5 Surprising Truths About Grief," by Ruth Davis Konigsberg, AARP.org

"Coping With Loss," TheAfterLoss.com

"Walking though Grief and Healing: Walking to Cope with Grief One Step at a Time," by Linda Wasmer Andrews, *PsychologyToday*.com.

Books

Finding Hope: Rediscovering Life After Tragedy by James Goll.

On Grief and Grieving: Finding the Meaning of Grief Through the Five Stages of Loss by Elizabeth Kubler Ross and David Kessler.

The Truth About Grief: The Myth of Its Five Stages and The New Science of Loss by Ruth Davis Konigsberg.

WALK ONE, DAY ONE

The LORD is close to the brokenhearted; he rescues those whose spirits are crushed. —Psalm 34:18 NLT

I took my first walk for this book on a day when my heart seemed broken and my spirit felt crushed. Nevertheless, I started walking, just putting one foot in front of the other.

I followed a road to a path past a meadow with aspen trees and bright yellow flowers. Their beauty lifted my spirit a little. I continued into a forest where I met other walkers and their dogs. I looked up and said hello. They returned my greetings and that lifted my spirit a little more.

I returned to my car with more strength and peace and I was able to go on with my day. This was when I realized how good walking is for me when I'm grieving.

You may be in pain now or maybe you're just feeling numb. Go out and take your first steps of the twenty-one days. You don't have to go for a long time, but you can if you like; whatever works for you.

After your walk, sit and write about your experience, focusing on how you felt before the walk and how you feel after it.

> Lord, help me feel your presence and your love with every step on this journey. Lift my spirit as we go. Amen.

~~~

Where you used to be, there is a hole in the world, which I find myself constantly walking around in the daytime, and falling in at night. I miss you like hell.

— Edna St. Vincent Millay

Your grief path is yours alone, and no one else can walk it, and no one else can understand it.

—Terri Irwin

RESOURCES

Videos:

God Will Take Care of You by Civilla D. Martin, performed by Antrim Mennonite Choir

You're Gonna Be Ok by Brian and Jenn Johnson

WALK TWO, DAY TWO

This is why I weep and my eyes overflow with tears. No one is near to comfort me, no one to restore my spirit...

— Lamentations 1:16 NIV

Old Testament people openly expressed their sorrow. The women wailed and the men tore their garments. Sometimes they covered themselves with ashes. They did all of this before the Lord.

What do New Testament people do? We tend to complain to each other. Or, we keep everything bottled up inside.

Lamenting is different from talking to a friend or a spouse or a counselor and different from the complaining we all tend to do; it's sharing our deepest feelings with Our Father and asking him our toughest questions. I'm told He likes it when we lament—it means we're in relationship—but He's not too fond of complaining.

The lament below begins with a dramatic statement about grief and ends with reasons to trust in God.

*The thought of my suffering and homelessness
is bitter beyond words.
I will never forget this awful time,
As I grieve over my loss.
Yet, still I dare to hope when I remember this:*

*The faithful love of the LORD never ends!
His mercies never cease.
Great is his faithfulness;
his mercies begin afresh each morning.*

— Lamentations 3:19-23 NLT

As you walk today, take a moment to talk with the Lord about your loss, and be honest with Him about how you feel.

Father, thank you for listening to me. Help me express my hurt and anger. Amen.

~~~

*For life and death are one, even as the river and the
sea are one.*

— Kahlil Gibran

RESOURCES

Video:
Cry Out to Jesus written and performed by Third Day

WALK THREE, DAY THREE

Blessed are those who mourn, for they will be comforted.

— Matthew 5:4 NIV

Many people, both locals and visitors, like to go along Clear Creek where it goes through Golden, Colorado. They're there even in the winter when the river freezes and the trees are decorated for Christmas.

When I was walking there one day, I saw a little boy and girl throwing twigs off the Billy Drew Bridge, under the watchful eye of their grandmother. They had it down: throw twig in, watch it go with the flow of the river downstream, throw another twig in, watch it go. Over and over. It was fun to watch them.

Then grieving me remembered something a widower said after his wife was ripped away from him and their children in a horrible accident: Grief makes you feel like a twig floating downstream through time.

His statement really resonated with me because I'd recently experienced being in shock after a tragedy. Does it resonate with you?

As you walk today, think about the analogy and whether you still feel that way.

> Thank you, Lord, for helping me face this loss by carrying me downstream of the event that caused it. Help me trust in You. Amen.

~~~

And can it be that in a world so full and busy the loss of one creature makes a void so wide and deep that nothing but the width and depth of eternity can fill it up!

— Charles Dickens, *The Mystery of Edwin Drood*

RESOURCES

Article:
"The Normal Physical and Mental Symptoms of Grief," VitasHealthcare.com.

Video:
Need You Now by Plumb

WALK FOUR, DAY FOUR

I lie in the dust; revive me by your word.

—Psalm 119:25 NLT

Grieving people often have the experience of being at a total loss of how to go forward on certain days. It helps at those times to simply focus on the Word of God.

I have found that doing so transforms my mind by renewing it, so I don't stay in the dust or sink into the mire of this world. Rather, I keep going in a good direction. I guess that's why the Lord advises, *Do not conform to the pattern of this world, but be transformed by the renewing of your mind* (Romans 12:2a NIV).

How do you focus on the Word? When you're walking, listen to a song with Scripture in it. Let it run through your mind again and again until you have it memorized or listen to a podcast of a Bible study. And, a low-tech way is to simply write down a passage of Scripture and read it when you take a break on your walk.

Today when you walk focus on a verse from the Bible. See how doing so affects your mind and heart.

> Lord, thank you for your Word. Thank you that it has the power to renew my mind and to transform me. Amen.

~~~

It often takes a tragedy to open our hearts, minds, and wills to the truth of God's Word.

—Rev. Billy Graham

Put your ear to the ground of God's word and listen to the rumble of his faithfulness coming.

—John Piper

RESOURCES

Video:
Thy Word performed by Amy Grant and Michael W. Smith

Bible studies:
Hope Sabbath School, HopeTV.org
You Version, YouVersion.com.

Peter D. Boddie photo.

WALK FIVE, DAY FIVE

Peace I leave with you, my peace I give you: I do not give to you as the world gives. Do not let your hearts be troubled and do not be afraid. —John 14:27 NIV

This Scripture saved my life when I was grieving my sister, who had killed herself. I was in my twenties and I remember sitting in my car on my lunch hour, memorizing it.

It spoke to me especially because I had just rocked my baby daughter to sleep at night and experienced being covered by a profound peace that was as tangible as a soft blanket. I was afraid, but my fear and trembling melted away in it. Later I heard about the peace that passes understanding and I knew that it was what I'd experienced. I came to love John 14:27.

Since then, I have grown and matured as a Christian and I now know that it was the Holy Spirit, the Comforter, who gave me that peace. Thank you, Lord.

As you walk today, ask the Lord for His peace.

Jesus, thank you for the peace that passes understanding. Holy Spirit, please comfort me and keep my heart from being troubled and fearful. Amen.

~~~

God cannot give us a happiness and peace apart from Himself, because it is not there. There is no such thing.

— C.S. Lewis

RESOURCES

Video:
Wonderful Peace by Warren D. Cornell, performed by the Mennonite Hour Men's Choir

Lyrics.
When peace like a river, attendeth my way,
When sorrows like sea billows roll
Whatever my lot, thou hast taught me to say
It is well, it is well, with my soul.

—Horatio Spafford, *It is Well With My Soul*

There's a peace far beyond understanding
May it ever set my heart at ease
Dare anxiety come I'll remember
That peace is a promise You keep
Peace is a promise You keep
—Hillsong Young & Free, *P E A C E*

WALK SIX, DAY SIX

He heals the brokenhearted and binds up their wounds.

— Psalm 147:3 NIV

Somebody once said to me, "We all lose our children." It seemed to me that this was an insensitive statement because, though most of us experience distance with our children at different times and to varying degrees, not all of us lose a child to sudden death. There's nothing like it, whether the child is a baby or a soldier at war or an adolescent killed in an accident; the pain is so enormous.

In another sense, there's a grain of truth in the statement; I mean, children grow up and move away or get lost to addiction or mental illness. There is sorrow then too, but it is a lesser grief while our children live.

It was on one of my trips from the airport, after saying goodbye to one of my children, that I was reminded that our Father in Heaven has also experienced the grief of losing a child, temporarily.

On another day I found a poignant book at the library, which depicted what it's like to lose a child. In *Rosalie Lightning* Tom Hart, a graphic novelist, memorialized his little daughter and showed his grief graphically. He wrote how walking was part of the grieving he and his wife did. "We walk. We walk circles around our friend Travis's sunny neighborhood."

His wife Leela remembered a "walking meditation" they did when they first met: Think 'yes' with every step when breathing in and then think 'thank you' with every step when breathing out. She wanted to do that meditation after the loss of their daughter. Tom wrote that he could do it, if he said his baby's name—Rosalie—when he exhaled instead of saying thank you.

On today's walk, try this meditation in your own way. Pick a word to focus on when you inhale and one to focus on when you exhale.

> Father, I don't understand the loss of a child, but You do. Help me to keep on going. Amen.

~~~

What do you do when you lose a child? You fall into a hole.

— Tom Hart

RESOURCES

Article:

"It is Well With My Soul: Historical Origins of the Hymn and the Tune," by David Depp

Books:

Rosalie Lightning by Tom Hart

Shattered: Surviving the Loss of a Child by Gary Roe

Lyrics:

> *What a friend we have in Jesus,*
> *All our sins and griefs to bear!*
> *What a privilege to carry*
> *Everything to God in prayer!*
>
> **—Joseph M. Scriven**

Videos:

Come as You Are by David Crowder

How Deep the Father's Love for Us by Stuart Townend

Website:

CompassionateFriends.org supports people who are grieving, especially after a child dies.

WALK SEVEN, DAY SEVEN

I look up to the mountains; does my strength come from mountains? No, my strength comes from God, who made heaven, and earth, and mountains.

— Psalm 121:1-2 MSG

I love to walk in the mountains. Paths along streams and through meadows and forests are comforting, but my favorites take me on the tundra, the land above timberline.

One day I went looking for signs of my sister in the Colorado mountains in the place where she died. I ended up crouching in the bushes, hiding from the evil that had caused her to commit suicide. (I guess it's just so hard to deal with the tragedy and the evil in some deaths.)

The Mexican holiday Dia Dos Muertas (Day of the Dead), is observed annually on October 31. It includes remembering ancestors and partying near their graves, even introducing babies to their deceased grandparents. Maybe it helps people deal with evil and death.

As the decades have gone by, I've learned how to fear less. What has helped me? Prayer and the promises and assurances of God. Isaiah 41:10 (TLB) says, *Fear not, for I am with you. Do not be dismayed. I am your God. I will strengthen you; I will help you; I will uphold you with my victorious right hand.*

As you walk today, focus on what God says He will do to help you, specifically. Also, you might think of someone who would pray for you, if you asked.

> Thank you, Father, that you are with me. Thank you for strengthening me and helping me as I grieve. Amen.

~~~

No one ever told me that grief felt so like fear. I am not afraid, but the sensation is like being afraid.

—C.S. Lewis

RESOURCES

Video:

I Am Not Alone by Kari Jobe

Lyrics:
> *There's a dark and a troubled side of life*
> *There's a bright and a sunny side too*
> *And tho' we meet with the darkness and strife*
> *The sunny side we also may view.*
>
> — Ada Blenkhorn

WALK EIGHT, DAY EIGHT

I am the good shepherd. The good shepherd lays down his life for the sheep. — John 10:11 NIV

I have a favorite walk by a river, the South Platte River, which is wide and shallow and mostly slow-moving, with quiet pools. A friend loves that same walk and used to grieve for a brother there. She found it comforting to stop on her walks, stand before the still waters for a moment and recite Psalm 23 in her mind.

> The Lord is my shepherd;
> I shall not want.
> He makes me to lie down in green pastures;
> He leads me beside the still waters.
> He restores my soul;
> He leads me in the paths of righteousness
> For His name's sake.

Yea, though I walk through the valley of the shadow of death,
I will fear no evil;
For You *are* with me;
Your rod and Your staff, they comfort me.

You prepare a table before me in the presence of my enemies;
You anoint my head with oil;
My cup runs over.
Surely goodness and mercy shall follow me
All the days of my life;
And I will dwell in the house of the Lord
Forever. (NKJV)

Do you hear promises in these beautiful verses?

As you start your walk today, exhale. Know that you are in good hands. Take a few moments in a quiet place to stop and remember or read Psalm 23.

Thank you, Lord, for your promises to be with me and protect me. Please walk with me today. Amen.

~~~

Healing takes courage, and we all have courage, even if we have to dig a little to find it.

—Tory Amos

RESOURCES

Videos:
The Lord is My Shepherd by Keith Green
The Lord is my Shepherd by Stuart Townend

WALK NINE, DAY NINE

Trust in the LORD forever, for the LORD, the LORD himself, is the Rock eternal. — Isaiah 26:4 NIV

While I was on vacation in Maine with my husband Peter, I walked at Acadia National Park. The path we followed wound from Sand Beach, up and around and over granite that had been at the edge of the Atlantic Ocean forever, taking the force of the waves every day. Yet, even that rock is not eternal; it will be worn away some day.

What a comfort to know we can rely on the Lord to be there always when life has changed and we're walking on the shifting sands of grief!

No, you say? How can I trust someone who took away what I loved most, who pulled the rug out from under me? What good is it to have God there forever, if He is not for me?

Perhaps it was not God who made it happen. Perhaps it was just natural law or even the evil one that did. In the story of Job, Satan destroyed Job's children and livestock and then made him sick. It seems God merely allowed Satan to ruin Job's life.

He *allowed* it? How could He?

Well, on your walk today, ask the Father to go with you and discuss this, just as Job did. Sit down after you walk and write down anything the Lord gives you, even impressions or ideas.

> Father, please walk with me today and give me your perspective on my situation in ways I can understand, in Jesus' Name. Amen.

~~~

Anyone can count the seeds in an apple, but only God can count the apples in a seed.

—Robert H. Schuller

RESOURCES

Article:
"Book of Job: Introduction to the Book of Job," Thoughtco.com

Video:
The Lord Taketh Away by Rebekah Rolland, performed by the Arizona Folk Ensemble

WALK TEN, DAY TEN

Jesus said to her, "I am the resurrection and the life. The one who believes in me will live, even though they die; and whoever lives by believing in me will never die. Do you believe this?" —John 11:25-26 NIV

Almost every day, a certain teacher walks down sidewalks and past crabapple trees growing in a straight line to a graveyard beyond them. She visits her son's grave and then goes home. This walk comforts her as she grieves.

One spring I felt compelled to paint the crabapple trees when they were in full bloom, including the graveyard in the picture. I hung the painting in a coffee shop with some other art and a card that told people how to get hold of me, if they wanted one of my paintings.

The teacher emailed me to say that she would like to buy the crabapple tree painting because her son was buried in the graveyard. I told her I wanted her to have it and to just pay me a little something. We agreed on a price and I took it to her.

I asked about her son. She told me he was only 17 and showed me his picture, which was next to a picture of his twin sister, but she didn't say how he died. I didn't ask.

I told her that the picture was painted from a squirrel's eye view. And then this came out of my mouth, "I realized after I painted it that the painting was about how resurrection life totally overwhelms death."

She leaned toward me with wide eyes. "That's what I thought it meant!"

When you walk today, think about this hope we have. Ask yourself, do I believe it?

> Lord, thank you that Resurrection Life will be so much greater than death. Help me remember that blessed hope in my heart and mind. Amen.

~~~

Our Lord has written the promise of resurrection, not in books alone, but in every leaf of springtime.

— Martin Luther

RESOURCES

Video:
Do it Again by Elevation Worship, Live

WALK ELEVEN, DAY ELEVEN

Let not your heart be troubled. You believe in God; believe also in me. In my Father's house are many mansions; if it were not so, I would have told you. I go to prepare a place for you. — John 14:1-2 NKJV

A thin, elderly man visited France and walked in a cemetery years after his military service took him to that country for duty. At the American Cemetery and Memorial in Normandy, he found a moment away from the tour group to visit his buddy's headstone.

His eyes welled up as he told the brother-in-arms whom he'd missed across the years what the world was like decades after they knew each other and what his own life had been. As he spoke, he was very aware that he got to live a full and long life when his friend didn't. He concluded, "I've never forgotten. See you in Heaven."

He straightened up, saluted and then walked away.

I imagine this is what my dad did when he visited the cemetery in Normandy for the fortieth anniversary of the landing on D-Day. (Later we visited the WWII Memorial in Washington, DC, together.)

Dad loved running and walking in the Colorado mountains. I now realize that those activities helped him with grieving, difficult memories and handling stress, and he taught me without words to use those activities for my grieving too. When Dad was dying I shared John 14:1–2 with him. He smiled when I read, "If it were not so, I would have told you."

On today's walk think about a memorial or cemetery you would like to visit to pay your respects as part of your journey through the long valley.

> Lord, direct my steps to places that will help me grieve and heal. Thank you for going with me. Amen.

~~~

Service before self, three words that define everyone who has ever worn the uniform. From one veteran to another: Never Forget.

— Dan Crenshaw, US Representative (R-Texas)

RESOURCES

Videos:
The Mansions of the Lord music by Nick Glennie-Smith

WALK TWELVE, DAY TWELVE

He heals the brokenhearted and binds up their wounds.

— Psalm 147:3 NIV

Sometimes the Lord heals us by placing friends in our lives who can walk with us through the valley.

My friend enjoyed being active and physically fit. Suddenly, her husband died of a heart attack. She was shocked and then beside herself with grief. She was brokenhearted for sure and wounded that life would take away a love she'd prayed for and waited for a long time.

During the early days after her loss, we walked around a nearby lake. Sometimes we walked in silence and sometimes she would share her struggles with the loss. I tried to empathize. It was an honor to walk with my friend and just be with her

Another friend found people who would go on hikes with him in the evenings after work and on weekends.

Linda Wasmer Andrews wrote for *Psychology Today* about the benefits of walking in times of grief, and specifically about the benefits of walking with friends, "Some people prefer to walk alone. But others appreciate the feeling of social connection that comes from striding shoulder-to-shoulder with another human being."

Is there a person in your life who knows what it is like to grieve, someone with whom you could walk? Think and pray about it on today's walk and then reach out to him or her.

> Lord, I could use a good friend or two to walk with me. Please bring us together. Amen.

~~~

People in grief need someone to walk with them without judging them.

— Gail Sheehy

RESOURCES

Article:
"Walking through Grief and Healing: Walking to Cope with Grief One Step at a Time," by Linda Wasmer Andrews

Video:
Since I Lost You by Phil Collins

WALK THIRTEEN, DAY THIRTEEN

Come to me all you who are weary and burdened, and I will give you rest. — Matthew 11:28 NIV

A friend of mine lost his son to suicide and then he lost his wife to cancer. He and his daughter—she'd lost a beloved brother and mother—faced a future that was devastatingly different from what they'd expected.

Some deaths are harder than others and some bereavements are too. It seemed to me that my friends could hardly see the sun at first, let alone imagine a way forward.

After some time went by, my friend told me they both reached out for professional help and that the psychiatrist they were seeing was a God send. He helped them face a future that looked so strange, by helping them address tough stuff that could have become roadblocks to successful grieving: difficult emotions, deep questions and trauma. They did their grief work and the future became a place of opportunity and possibilities for both, with God.

Here's one little way of dealing with tough stuff that I've found helpful, a meditation from the GriefinCommon.com blog. Think of a painful part of your loss and then repeat to yourself, out loud or in your mind, I had no control over what happened, and keep saying it until you feel a weight lift off you. Repeat with other painful aspects of your loss.

Another thing that has helped me is writing about the tough stuff in a journal; putting it down on paper allows me to get it out of my mind.

Try the mediation as you walk today or take 15 minutes to write down the tough stuff that is bothering you.

> Lord, help me with the tough stuff, so I don't get stuck in the valley. Lead me to help, if I need it. Amen.

~~~

The rip in my heart will become a scar, a permanent reminder of how loved you are.

—Helen Fosberg

RESOURCES

Article:
"Grief Roadblocks and How to Let Go of Tough Emotions," GriefinCommon.com

Video:
Tell Your Heart to Beat Again written by Bernie Herms, Randy Phillips and Matthew West, performed by Danny Gokey

WALK FOURTEEN, DAY FOURTEEN

But they that wait upon the Lord shall renew their strength; they shall mount up with wings as eagles; they shall run, and not be weary; and they shall walk, and not faint. — Isaiah 40:31 KJV

A man takes a walk to a river with his fly-fishing gear where he used to fish with his father, who has died. He wades into the water and begins to cast. He focuses not on his grief, but on the sounds of the river and the way his line snaps out with a flick of his wrist. He savors the peace and quiet at the river and feels his strength returning.

I walk near red rocks close to my home. I stop to rest in a pavilion with a great view. As I sit there, western bluebirds come and fly back and forth. I'm delighted and thank the Lord; I love bluebirds! They're a joy to me and focusing on them lifts my spirit.

Speaking of birds, sometimes when I'm inside my house I hear the buzz of hummingbird wings outside. which causes me to go out and look for them. If I see them, I feel hope even on days when I've been weighed down with grief.

How can grief and the bluebirds and hummingbirds exist at the same time? Good question. All I know is that, as I choose to focus more on the birds and less on the grief, I can go on, live and love life.

Today as you walk, take a break from your grief and just focus on your surroundings.

> Father, thank you for renewing my strength in ways I don't expect. Help me trust you and let my grief diminish. Amen.

~~~

The mind has its own harmony, its own way of regaining balance and stability after a loss.

—Rodney Smith, MSW

RESOURCES

Videos:

Praise You in This Storm written by Bernie Herms and Mark Hall, performed by Casting Crowns.

Notting Hill scene where William (Hugh Grant) walks through four seasons of grieving, emerges on the other side

WALK FIFTEEN, DAY FIFTEEN

Trust in the Lord with all your heart, and do not lean on your own understanding. In all your ways acknowledge him, and he will make straight your paths.

— Proverbs 3:5-6 ESV

A woman who had lost a loved one in a plane crash reminded me to look up as I walk. She said that when she looked at the Earth, she could barely take another step, barely breathe, but when she looked up she found hope.

Do you think her loved one would want her to be hopeful as she goes on living?

Before my dear friend died of ovarian cancer, she gave her husband permission to remarry and she instructed her daughter to accept this. It was clear what she wanted for him.

Before my close cousin died of breast cancer, she prepared her two sons, her husband and her parents to go on and live without her. I'm sure she wanted them to be as happy as they could be after she was gone.

I ask myself: What would the loved ones I've lost want for me as I go on in this world? None of them ever said in so many words. Nevertheless, because I knew them, I know the answer; they would want me to live life fully and be happy.

As you walk today, ask yourself that question: What would my loved one(s) want for me as I survive in this world?

> Thank you, Father, for making my paths straight as I trust You. Help me live my best life. Amen.

~~~

How lucky I am to have something that makes it so hard to say goodbye.

— Winnie the Pooh

*Life is not about waiting for the storms to pass . . .
It's about learning how to dance in the rain.*
—Vivian Greene

RESOURCES

Video:
Friends by Michael W. Smith

WALK SIXTEEN, DAY SIXTEEN

I have told you these things, so that in me you may have peace. In this world you will have trouble. But take heart! I have overcome the world. — John 16:33 NIV

Sometimes grief will ambush you. It may happen early on when you're coming out of shock or it may happen years out from your loss, if something new comes to light or you experience a sight or a sound or a smell that triggers a memory.

I remember instances of both. On an ordinary day after my sister Cindy died, I was in the grocery store. *Annie's Song* by John Denver came over the sound system as I was picking out oranges. This was the song played at my sister's wedding, when I was her maid of honor. Hearing it ambushed me, nearly knocking me down, and I had to leave the store.

When I was coming up to the 34-year anniversary (Yes, 34 *years*!) of her death I realized what the first domino was in the long line of events that led to Cindy's death. My grief and anger were intense. It was days of hard grieving and I dropped out of the world for a short time. I had to forgive some people again and ask the Lord to help me forgive.

I know the pain of that loss is never going to be gone from my life completely. It's always going to be part of who I am, and it might show up from time to time. I will just have to feel it and then let it go as I continue to try to live the best life I can.

Today as you walk, prepare yourself for the contingency that you may have days when you'll be ambushed by grief. Make up your mind that, if it happens, you'll grieve a little, let the grief go, get up and keep going.

> Lord, sometimes grief sneaks up on me and I can barely stand. Please be there to hold me up and help me get back up. Amen.

Death is the sound of distant thunder at a picnic.

— W.H. Auden

RESOURCES

Video:
Just Be Held by Casting Crowns

WALK SEVENTEEN, DAY SEVENTEEN

My help comes from the LORD, the Maker of heaven and earth. — Psalm 121:2 NIV

If you believe we are created in God's image then you must know that we are meant to be creative; I mean, our Father is the Great Creator. So, we can use creativity to heal when we're grieving.

I've been a writer and photographer, but after my mother died, I went to a charity event where we were sipping wine and painting. I discovered that I had a little of the family talent for painting. (No. I had *never* painted a picture ever.) The fact that I could paint made me laugh, and I started healing through painting.

Also, music has been a friend in my walk through the long valley; specifically, I have learned to play the mandolin, and the fiddle. My dad gave me the mandolin before he died, probably because my sister played it.

There were two violins in his collection too. I became caretaker of them, so they wouldn't get damaged in a storage unit and, after his death I took fiddle lessons on one of them.

When my mom was dying, I asked the Lord for a place to sing and he impressed me to go sing with a local choir at a church. Singing was a great comfort, as were the kind brothers and sisters in the choir.

When you walk today, think about how creativity has been, or could be, a part of your grieving and healing.

> Lord, thank you for making us in Your Image. Help us to create and heal as you do. Amen.

Grief provides some of the low notes of our lives that make it a richer symphony overall.

—Dr. Shelley Carson

RESOURCES

Article:
"The Creativity of Grief," by Abi May

Video:
This is My Father's World by Franklin L. Sheppard, performed by Fernando Ortega

WALK EIGHTEEN, DAY EIGHTEEN

*And provide for those who grieve in Zion—
to bestow on them a crown of beauty
　instead of ashes,
the oil of joy
　instead of mourning,
and a garment of praise
　instead of a spirit of despair.* — Isaiah 61:3 NIV

There will come a time in the long valley when it's right to focus on walking out of it.

When this time comes along for you, remember that Jesus walked out of the tomb and the Lord will give you what you need to do it too.

What does that mean? Each person might have to discover the meaning for himself or herself. However, consider this: you've been exercising your power to choose where to put your focus at any time, on tragedy and loss or on the life, beauty and hope that remain. Maybe that's key.

Some days it will be natural to focus on the losses you have endured, other days you can focus on what you want your life to look like in the future or on helping other people who are hurting. Be assured that you are not abandoning your loved one(s) by thinking of other things.

On today's walk, turn your mind to something besides your grief: a hobby, a pet, work, church, friends or family.

> Lord, I'm counting on you to take care of my loved ones. Help me focus on my life more and more. Amen.

~~~

You cannot prevent the birds of sorrow from flying over your head, but you can prevent them from building nests in your hair.

— Old Chinese Proverb

RESOURCES

Article:
"Grief and the Fear of Letting Go," What's Your Grief (WYG) blog

Video:
He Gives Beauty for Ashes written by Crystal Lewis, who performs with Ron Kenoly.

WALK NINETEEN, DAY NINETEEN

He has made everything beautiful in its time.

— Ecclesiastes 3:11 NIV

Beauty. It's so healing, especially when you're grieving, and it helps us to connect with the life around us and to realize that we are still part of that life, even after tragedy and loss.

When I was grieving the death of my mother, the Lord led me to a safe place—a botanic gardens—where beauty was all around. What a gift. I walked and walked there. Do you have such a place near you where the natural beauty takes your breath away and even takes you out of time?

Some of my favorite places are the valleys in the mountains of Colorado where wildflowers grow and the high country above timberline. Another favorite place is

Prince Edward Island, Canada, where red sand beaches meet the waters of the gulf of St. Lawrence. Still another is Oregon by the ocean; I just love the sound of the waves breaking and the vastness of the ocean.

Vacations in beautiful places around the world offer opportunities for unforgettable walks. Maybe you could plan such a trip during your 21 days.

If you can, go to one of your favorite beautiful places to walk today. Drink it in with all your senses. Listen to your beautiful music on the way there or as you walk.

> Thank you, Lord, for showing me beauty every day. Help me perceive it. Amen.

~~~

Beauty is the gift of God.

— Thomas Aquinas

I don't think of all the misery, but of all the beauty that remains.

— Anne Frank

RESOURCES

Article:
"Finding Beauty in Grief," by Carol Eckl

Video: *Daystar Reflections Complete Video Montage*

WALK TWENTY, DAY TWENTY

And we know that in all things God works for the good of those who love him, who have been called according to his purpose. — Romans 8:28 NIV

Has anyone suggested to you that you should focus on the good times with your loved ones?

I was having a bad time on the anniversary of the death of my sister when a friend made that suggestion to me on social media. Good idea, I thought. I realized I hadn't consciously tried it, maybe because I feared it would be too painful, maybe because grief kept me connected.

So, I went out and took a walk with my husband and, on purpose, we started remembering the good times with loved ones who have gone away. We talked about his mother and father, my father and grandmother, and his older brother. Pretty soon our walk was over, and we had barely begun remembering the good times, but it felt good.

There are other things to do that will help you feel positive and hopeful, when you are ready to go there. (Thank you to Dr. Daniel Amen for suggesting people pass them along.)

- Say each morning that it will be a great day.
- Plan in one purposeful activity for each day.
- Think of three things during each day for which you're grateful. Thank the Lord.
- Each night think about three things that went well during the day. Thank the Lord.

As you walk today, spend some time remembering the good times with your loved one(s).

> Lord, help me remember good things and please make the difficult memories, trauma and pain fade. Amen.

~~~

The people you lose remain a part of you. Remember them and always cherish the good moments spent with them.

— Christopher Walken

RESOURCES

Article:
"Getting Through Grief and Letting Go," by Angela Morrow, RN

Book:
Feel Better Fast and Make it Last by Dr. Daniel Amen

WALK TWENTY ONE, DAY TWENTY ONE

Cast your cares on the LORD and he will sustain you; he will never let the righteous be shaken.

—Psalm 55:22 NIV

Count on the Lord to be there with you as you walk out of the long valley. (No. You *won't necessarily* be ready because you've come to this last devotion.) When you're getting close there is something you can do to make it easier: Create a tribute to your loved one(s); it will be a place where you can anchor your memory of them while you go on with life.

What can you do as a tribute? It can be as traditional as creating a headstone for a gravesite or it may be something unusual. Each person's tributes will be different, but once you create one, it should be easier to walk out of the long valley of grief without feeling you are abandoning your loved one.

Here are some ideas: Buy a memorial brick or plaque for a bench at a botanical garden where you walk; contribute to organizations that fight diseases that have taken loved ones; create some kind of living memorial, such as singing in a choir or playing an instrument as a memorial to a musical loved one.

I've created various tributes for my different loved ones who have gone. They have helped me move on and continue living.

On today's walk, think about what would be meaningful to you as a tribute to your loved one(s). After your walk, write down first steps to making the tribute happen.

> Thank you, Lord, that I can go on living and still honor and remember precious ones who are gone. Amen.

~~~

When they died, you didn't stop loving them and they didn't stop loving you.

— David Kessler

RESOURCES

Video:
You'll Never Walk Alone, composed by Richard Rogers and Oscar Hammerstein II, performed by Celtic Woman

AFTERWORD

He will wipe every tear from their eyes. There will be no more death or mourning or crying or pain, for the old order of things has passed away.
— Revelation 21:4 NIV

How do we have this promise, this blessed hope? I'd be remiss if I didn't write the reason. It's because of what Jesus did for humanity, giving *his* life so that we could have *eternal* life. Praise and honor and glory be to the Lord!

Jesus was a man of sorrows and acquainted with grief (Isaiah 53:3); he suffered and he understands our suffering. No wonder the revelation by and about him would promise to wipe away our tears and take away our pain.

If you feel so led, the end of this twenty-one days would be a good time for you to reconnect in relationship with Jesus or to receive his gift of salvation for the first time. You don't have to change anything about yourself, or join a church, just focus your heart and mind on Him and pray the following:

> Jesus, I repent of all my sins. Come into my heart and cleanse me. Thank you for your sacrifice. I make you the Lord of my life. Amen.

Hopefully, this devotional has helped you on your journey through the long valley. I don't expect your journey is over yet; please feel free to return to the first walk and go through the twenty-one days again, or find another devotional and read it before you walk.

God bless you. Walk on!

www.ingramcontent.com/pod-product-compliance
Lightning Source LLC
Chambersburg PA
CBHW071222070526
44584CB00019B/3122